READ and LEARN™

Activity

FAVORITE BIBLE STORIES

STICKER & ACTIVITY BOOK

ISBN 979-8-225-02621-9
10 9 8 7 6 5 4 3 2 1 26 27 28 29 30
Design by Maria Lilja
Printed in Guangzhou, China

Scholastic Inc., 557 Broadway, New York, NY 10012
Scholastic UK Ltd., Bosworth Avenue, Warwick, CV34 6UQ
Scholastic LTD, Unit 89E, Lagan Road, Dublin Industrial Estate, Glasnevin, Dublin 11 HP5F

Little Shepherd® BOOKS

God's Garden

After God created the world, He planted the Garden of Eden. He made all kinds of trees for the garden and put Adam, the man He had made, there to look after it. God saw that it was not good for Adam to be alone. He filled the garden with every kind of bird and animal. Adam named them all. God also made a woman to be Adam's partner and wife. Adam called her Eve.

USE STICKERS TO FINISH THE PICTURE.

The Great Flood

God filled the world with beautiful and amazing things, but the people forgot about God. One man named Noah obeyed God. God told Noah, "I want you to build a great ark for yourself and your family. Bring into the ark two of every animal." Noah did as God asked, and his family and all the animals were saved.

HOW MANY ANIMALS CAN YOU NAME IN THIS PICTURE?

FIND AND CIRCLE THE WORDS IN THE PUZZLE!

NOAH
ARK
ZEBRA
RHINO
PIG
BIRD

G	D	L	T	N	Z	I
Q	I	O	D	O	E	A
S	R	P	R	A	B	R
W	G	H	X	H	R	K
K	J	P	I	R	A	G
Q	G	Q	D	N	O	M
J	B	I	R	D	O	Z

Joseph the Dreamer

Jacob lived in the land of Canaan with twelve sons, including Joseph. Jacob loved Joseph very much and gave him a fancy coat for his birthday, which made Joseph's brothers jealous.

God gave Joseph the gift of seeing into the future through his dreams. One of these dreams was of wheat bundles bowing down to his own bundle of wheat.

COLOR JOSEPH'S COAT!

Color by Number

- **1 = Red**
- **2 = Orange**
- **3 = Green**
- **4 = Blue**
- **5 = Purple**

USE STICKERS TO FINISH THE PICTURE.

How many bundles of wheat are bowing down to the bundle in the center? Circle the right answer.

8 10 11

A Baby in a Basket

To keep him safe from an evil new king, baby Moses' mother put him in a basket and placed him in the Nile River. The king's daughter was bathing in the river and heard the baby crying. She raised Moses as her son and kept him safe.

Can you help baby Moses float safely from his mother to the king's daughter?

Food in the Desert

After escaping Egypt, the Israelites began to run out of food. Moses asked God for help. The next morning, after the dew had dried, thick white flakes were left behind on the ground. This bread was called "manna."

Trace the word MANNA.

MANNA

Now write the word MANNA on your own.

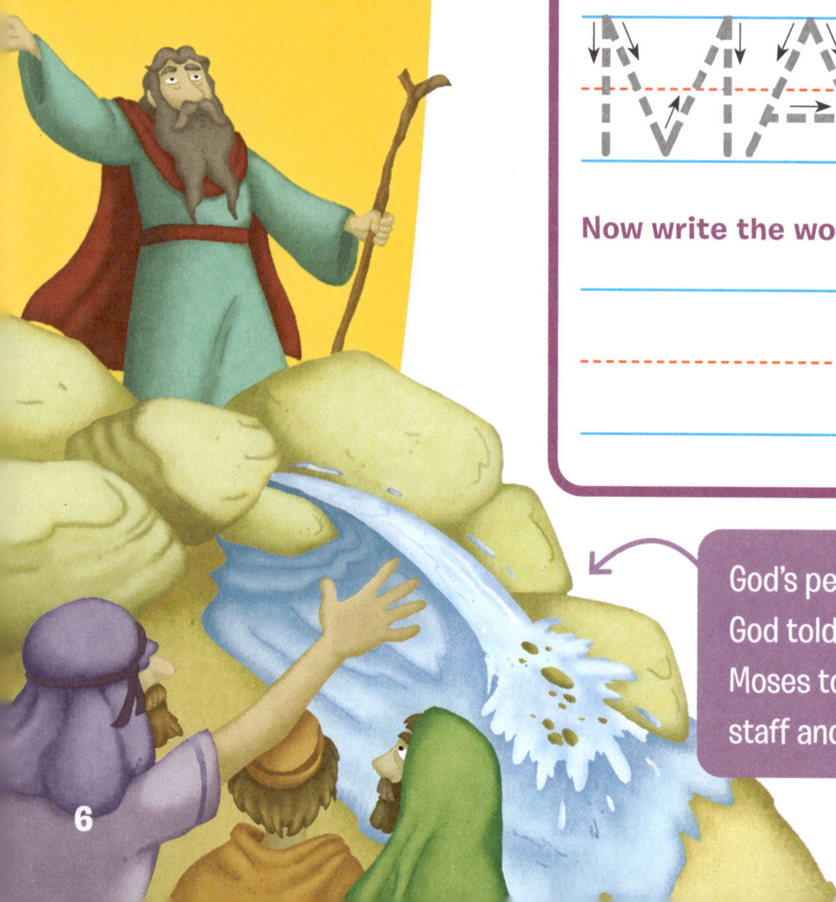

God's people needed water too. God told Moses to go to a big rock. Moses touched the rock with his staff and water began to flow out.

Samson

CONNECT THE DOTS TO FINISH THE PILLARS AND THEN COLOR!

God sent Samson to lead His people. He gave Samson superhuman strength — as long as he did not cut his hair. One day, Samson told a woman named Delilah his secret. She told the Philistines and when Samson fell asleep, they cut off Samson's braids.

Samson prayed to God to make him strong again. At last, he had a chance to get back at his enemies and pushed the pillars that were holding up many Philistines. Samson was a hero to God's people.

David and Goliath

Goliath was a giant who scared everyone in the Israelite army. A young shepherd named David believed he could defeat him with God's help. Goliath had armor and a large sword. David had just a sling and five smooth stones. When Goliath taunted him, David took aim and shot a stone at the giant. The stone hit Goliath in the forehead, and he fell to the ground! David had saved the Israelites.

FIND AND CIRCLE THE WORDS IN THE PUZZLE!

ARMOR
GIANT
DAVID
ARMY
STONE
SLING

G	I	A	N	T	A	G
Q	D	O	D	D	R	S
S	N	X	A	I	M	T
D	A	V	I	D	O	O
K	X	W	Y	R	R	N
G	W	A	R	M	Y	E
O	S	L	I	N	G	T

Elisha and the Widow's Oil

A woman whose husband had died came to Elisha for help. She needed money but only had one small bottle of olive oil. Elisha told the woman to ask her neighbors for their empty jars. Then Elisha told her to pour the olive oil from her bottle into the jars, one at a time. The woman poured oil into the first jar and filled it up. With her one small bottle of oil, she filled every jar in the house with oil left over!

Daniel and the Lions

Write the numbers 1, 2, and 3 in the order each event happened.

King Darius trusted Daniel, but some jealous men used his faith in God to try to get rid of him. They asked the king to make a law against praying to anyone but the king, or the person would be thrown in a pit of hungry lions. Daniel was caught praying!

The king had no choice. "I am sorry," he said. "I pray that your God will rescue you." The next morning, Daniel was safe! The king ordered his people to honor the God of Daniel.

Use the clues to fill in the puzzle.

ACROSS

2. What were people forbidden to do with the new law?

4. Who was thrown in the pit?

DOWN

1. Another word for "trust."

2. Where did the king live?

3. What kind of animals were in the pit?

4. What was the king's name?

Queen Esther

King Xerxes had a beautiful and good wife named Esther. She was a Jew. A bad man named Haman wanted to get rid of Esther's cousin Mordecai — and all the Jews. Esther was brave and went to the king and asked for her people to be saved. The king loved Esther and immediately made a new law that the Jews could defend themselves. They honored the king and Queen Esther.

USE STICKERS TO FINISH THE PICTURE.

Did you know?
Palace rules said no one could approach the king without permission. Esther was brave and he agreed to speak with her! She saved the Jewish people.

Jonah and the Big Fish

Color the picture! Then add fish stickers to the ocean.

God told Jonah to go to Nineveh to tell the people to stop doing bad things, but Jonah didn't want to go. He got on a boat to try to run away from God! During the trip, a storm came up. Everyone thought the storm was Jonah's fault, so Jonah said to throw him into the sea. God sent a big fish to swallow him, where he was safe for three days and nights. The fish then spat Jonah out on the shore.

Jesus Is Born

Many years ago, Jesus was born in a stable full of animals. Wise men from the east came to honor Him.

An angel from the Lord told Joseph, Jesus' father, that Jesus was in trouble, and they had to escape to Egypt. When Jesus was a child, His parents found Him in the temple one day, sitting with the teachers and asking questions. Jesus later became a carpenter. He was a special man whose life was about to change.

What Happened Next? Write the numbers 1, 2, 3, 4, and 5 in the order each event happened.

USE STICKERS
TO ADD ANIMALS
IN THE STABLE.

Twelve Men

USE STICKERS TO FINISH THE PICTURE.

Jesus traveled around, telling people, "Turn back to God!" One day, He was walking along the lakeshore and saw two brothers, Peter and Andrew. Jesus said, "Come with me. I will teach you how to bring in people instead of fish." Jesus continued to call men to follow Him. They were called His disciples and Jesus taught them God's Word.

How many disciples did Jesus have?

10 11 12

Jesus the Healer

Jesus healed many people during His time on earth. He told fevers to go away. He healed a skin disease called leprosy. He healed people's legs so they could walk! Jesus once put mud on the eyes of a man who was blind from birth and then he could see. The people were amazed at Jesus' miracles.

Draw lines to connect the rhyming words.

COLUMN 1	COLUMN 2
Head	Eyes
Heal	Touch
Hurt	Dirt
Rise	Bed
Crutch	Feel

A Storm

One night, after Jesus had been teaching, He said, "Let's travel to the other side of the lake." Before long, a giant storm rolled in. The waves crashed over the sides of the boat and began to fill it with water! Jesus lifted His arms and faced the gusting wind and the splashing waves. "Quiet!" He said to the wind. "Be still!" The wind stopped and the waves became calm.

Spot the Difference! Circle the picture that is different. Point out the differences.

Count the number of items in each picture and write it on the line.

Birds: ______

Seeds: ______

Plants: ______

Pears: ______

A Very Important Story

Jesus taught the people about God. Jesus told a story about a farmer planting seeds. Some seeds were eaten by birds and some grew on rocks and died. But the seeds that landed in good soil grew tall and strong, making lots of fruit! Jesus said the seeds are like God's Word. Some people don't accept God's Word, but those who do can share it with others and help it grow!

Bread and Fish for Everyone

A huge crowd had gathered to hear Jesus teach. But there was no food for the people as night fell. A child had a basket with only five loaves of bread and two fish. Jesus thanked God for the food and began dividing it up among the disciples. As the disciples handed out food to the crowd, there was enough for everyone!

Finish the pattern!

Color the picture!

Jesus Blesses the Children

In one place where Jesus and the disciples traveled, people brought their children. They wanted Jesus to place His hands on the children and bless them. The disciples told the people to stop bothering Jesus. But Jesus said, "Let the children come to me! People who are like these little children belong to the Kingdom of God."

A Joyful Sunday

After Jesus died on Friday, He was buried in a tomb with a stone rolled over the front. On Sunday morning, some women who followed Jesus went to the tomb. To their amazement, Jesus' body was gone! Suddenly, two men in shining white clothes stood beside them. "Jesus isn't here. He has risen from death."

Color by Number

1 = Red
2 = Yellow
3 = Green
4 = Blue
5 = Purple

Jesus Is Taken to Heaven

After Jesus rose from the dead, He stayed with His disciples for forty days. He spoke with them about God's kingdom. "Tell everyone in the world about me." Suddenly a cloud appeared over their heads. Then, right before their eyes, Jesus was taken up into the sky.

Find and circle the words in the puzzle!

CLOUD
DISCIPLE
HEAVEN
JESUS
KINGDOM
POWER
RETURN
SPIRIT

D	P	O	W	E	R	M	O	F	N
R	E	T	U	R	N	L	A	P	F
R	X	M	S	C	L	O	U	D	J
O	H	U	O	L	J	W	S	T	L
A	E	T	T	D	X	E	I	N	A
O	A	H	K	M	G	R	S	T	O
D	V	L	R	S	I	N	N	U	V
O	E	N	K	P	P	K	I	R	S
Y	N	I	S	O	W	R	P	K	I
P	X	D	I	S	C	I	P	L	E

God Loves You!

Jesus taught everyone about God's love.

Draw a picture of things you love and are thankful for.

ADD STICKERS TOO!

Stickers for activities on pages 1-12.

Stickers for activities on pages 13–24.

Stickers for Noah's Ark activity.

After the great flood, God sent a beautiful rainbow!
Use stickers to finish the scene!